Mess

Michael Wagner
Gaston Vanzet

Rigby®

www.Rigby.com
1-800-531-5015

Rigby Focus Forward

This Edition © 2009 Rigby, a Harcourt Education Imprint

Published in 2006 by Nelson Australia Pty Ltd ACN: 058 280 149
A Cengage Learning company

1 2 3 4 5 6 7 8 374 14 13 12 11 10 09 08 07
Printed and bound in China

The Mess
ISBN-13   978-1-4190-3677-4
ISBN-10   1-4190-3677-7

THE Mess

Michael Wagner
Gaston Vanzet

Contents

Not Happy

Mom was not happy.
She was not happy at all.

"No going out!" she said.
"No friends over! No TV! No fishing!
Not until you have cleaned up
this mess!"

Mom wanted me to clean up my room.
She wanted me to clean it up NOW!

But how do you clean a room?
First you get a broom!

The Broom

I got the broom.
I looked for some floor to sweep.
I looked all around.
Where was the floor?

My floor was not there.
It was lost under ...

The MESS!

There was no floor to sweep,
so I did not need the broom.
I had to get rid of the broom.
I went to my closet.
It was hard to open
since the mess was in the way.

I put the broom in the closet
since it was empty.

Chapter 3

The Closet

Now what do I do?

"That's it!" I said.
"The closet
is empty.
That is where
the mess can go!"

In went a hat,

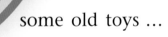

some old toys ...

and
my lunch.

I was happy to see
some of the floor again.
The closet was
a big help.

I put some
more things in
the closet.
In went a shoe,

some books,

and my shorts.

I did not stop there.
In went more shoes, my TV,
and the cat—maybe not the cat.
In went *all* of my things!
It was good to be clean.

Then the mess was gone.
All I had to do now
was shut the closet doors.

Chapter 4

Not a Good Idea

I leaned on the doors.
I leaned back hard.
I could not shut them.

Mom came in.
She looked around my room.

"Jack!" she said.
"What a good cleanup!
Now all you have to do
is sweep the floor."

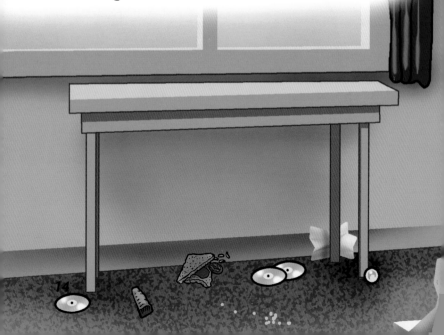

"I can do that, Mom," I said.
"I will just get the broom
out of the closet."

That was not a good idea.